T0199197

AuthorHouse™
1663 Liberty Drive
Bloomington, IN 47403
www.authorhouse.com
Phone: 1 (800) 839-8640

This book is printed on acid-free paper.

ISBN: 978-1-7283-2719-8 (sc)
ISBN: 978-1-7283-2718-1 (e)

Print information available on the last page.

Published by AuthorHouse 09/11/2019

authorHOUSE®

BEYOND COPING

PART ONE
JOURNEY TO PARADISE

As the first anniversary of the fire approaches, I am reflecting on not only the events that have unfolded over the past months, but also on my transformation. Who I was before the fire does not resemble the person I am today. I have truly buried my former self in the ashes left by the fire In Paradise. In eight months, through meditation and extensive reading I have evolved into a stronger, self-assured woman. I had to not only survive, I had to forge ahead with determination and optimism. I couldn't just cope with what had happened to me; I had to rise above the impact of the fire and find new meaning to my life.

My journey began in January 2018. I was living in Southern California with my fiancé. Everything in my life was on track: I was working as an Independent Study Coordinator at an Adult Education School. I also was a Sociology professor at a nearby community college. I had been there for over twenty years. Both jobs were fulfilling to me and I was so fortunate to be able to get paid for what I loved doing. At 68, and in good health, life was pretty rosy for me.

In January, my fiancé discussed with me the possibility of moving up to Northern California. He had been estranged from his grown kids for some time and he wanted to now be closer to them. I was nervous about the prospect of moving as I would not know anyone and I did not know if I could procure employment. I would be leaving the familiar behind me and going into the unknown. A couple we knew in the park where we lived had recently moved to Paradise. Jim was familiar with the town and suggested that we check it out.

We ended up purchasing a home in Magalia, just outside of Paradise. It took 6 months for all the paper work to go through and in May we were able to move half of our belongings into our new home. I struggled with trying to find room for all my "stuff". I had an extensive wardrobe, complete with hats, multiple jewelry sets, coats and footwear. I had also accumulated many books, pictures, and antiques. But there was not enough room in the house for everything. The closets were tiny, and I could not cram everything into them. Looking back, I can't believe that finding room for everything was one of biggest concerns!

We were to make the final trip to Paradise the first week in July. Then the unthinkable happened. Jim suffered a major heart attack a couple of days before we were to make the move. Both major arteries were blocked and stents were put in. I was left to finish packing and hire young men to drive the U-Haul.

We settled into our home for the next couple of months. Jim made some improvements on the house and I procured a job as a substitute teacher and began work at the end of August. Jim went back to Southern California the last week In August to do some work.

Everything was falling into place. I joined a book club, met some new friends, and was just beginning to explore the town of Paradise. Jim was able to go bowling and fishing and he found a therapist. I was glad we made the decision to make the journey to Paradise. Jim and I were planning to go to Canada for Christmas to see my mother.

PRELUDE TO THE FIRE

So just when I think my life is on track, I am derailed! I had been working for a week and was making all kinds of plans for the next month. Then I get the phone call that my mother in Canada had fallen and broken her hip. She had tripped on an area rug in the hallway, and was on the floor for almost 5 hours before she was rescued by the landlady. Our new neighbors drove me to the airport in Sacramento and I made it to the hospital at midnight. I was extremely worried because she had broken her other hip 3 years earlier and she was still recovering. She was almost 95 years old.

She declined rehab and told the doctor she wanted to recover at home. She couldn't walk; she needed a bedpan, and she had to have shots in her stomach for the next 20 days. I was shown how to administer the shots, and the doctor released her into my care. I was quite apprehensive about the task of being her caretaker; I had no experience in tending to other people. But I managed to arrange for transportation to bring her home and stayed with her for 6 weeks.

While I was tending to her physical needs, I reflected on the book I treasured "Tuesdays with Morrie." Morrie was inflicted with Lou Gehrig's disease and was worried about having someone to tend to his bathing and bathroom needs. But he overcame his anxiety by posing the observation that adults love to bathe babies and to wrap them in warm blankets; but, as adults, we are repulsed by the idea of having to bathe another adult. Morrie now surrendered to being bathed by his wife and nurse. Mother was mortified that her daughter was going to wipe her butt until I told her it was an opportunity to take care of her as she took care of me.

Mother told me she did not just want to "cope" with her situation. She did not want to wallow in self-pity. While in the hospital, the nurses wrote on the white board "only positive thoughts allowed." She stated that she was not specific in her stating her desires to Abraham (Law of Attraction). She had visualized a wonderful vacation with me where she would not have to cook, clean or make beds. Her mistake was, she didn't mention that it was to take place in Vegas! So she got her vacation in a different place! So now she visualized being healed and she was going to use her recovery time as a blessing to be with her daughter. She decided that everything happens for a reason and the reason she fell was to bring me home and spend time with her! So we made the 6 weeks mother and daughter spa time!

I was able to cook her favorite meals; every night we had frozen yogurt with bananas and chocolate syrup. I would massage her feet, wrapping them in essential oils. We discussed the law of attraction and not allowing any toxic thoughts get in the way of her recovering.

Finally it was time for me to return to Paradise. Before I left, mother had given me special family heirlooms, and beautiful pieces of clothing. I felt truly blessed.

Once home, I immediately went back to work. I was able to substitute for three weeks. Jim found a part-time job just down the street from where we lived. It was perfect for him. He was so excited to be doing something useful with his life again. He even started bowling once a week with his friend Ken and bought a fishing license and gear. Once again we were on track. He finished working on the back deck and we were planning on redoing the fireplace. Life was good.

THE FIRE

November 8, 2018

Jim and I sat on our back deck drinking coffee as we did every morning. Jim was going to go to therapy in a couple of hours and then to his new job. So far, he had only worked 4 hours as he just got hired. We noticed a red patch in the sky, but it seemed to be quite a distance away. I left for Pine Ridge Elementary where I was to teach until 11:30. Just as school was beginning, a number of parents came to the school to pick up their children. Around 8:30, we were told to go to the cafeteria. On the way there, the air was thick with smoke. Most of the children were picked up by 9:30 and we loaded up the rest of them on buses to take us to another school where we would be safe. I still had 4 students from my class. There were already many cars on the road, trying to get out of town. We reached Cedarwood School where we were told we would have to evacuate from there also. We picked up some high school students and a group of special ed students.

Inside the bus was somewhat like a cocoon shielding us from the chaos outside – cars trying to merge from the side streets, at times, cutting us off; cars now stranded by the side of the road, people screaming and the rapidly approaching flames behind us.

I kept trying to contact the parents and guardians of my four students to let them know they were okay. The special needs children were shielded from the view of the flames and I would sing to them and feed them snacks from their backpacks. But the high school students were visibly distraught: one male student started screaming and crying when he got a text that his neighbor's house burnt down. He couldn't reach his parents and I tried to calm him down. It was a long four hours to reach Chico – when normally it would have taken us 20 minutes. Traffic was backed up for miles. The flames in the sky seemed to be looming all around us.

Finally we arrived at a church In Chico. I couldn't believe how organized the community was: Tables were set up to get names of everyone coming in; there were separate rooms for each school; the main room was set up for families and their pets who had to evacuate their home. Businesses donated food (pizzas, sandwiches, chips), drinks, games, clothing, and blankets. I kept busy, helping with the food and supervising the children. I didn't have any time to think about my own personal plight. I knew that Jim had safely evacuated and he had rescued my cat.

Around 6 o'clock, Jim's daughter-in-law- Dawn picked me up. Once I sat down in the vehicle and we were on the way to her house, I started to feel numb. I still couldn't fathom everything that was going on. In the back of my mind, I was certain our house was safe – it was further away from Paradise so I was certain the fire would not go that far. I did not know how serious the fire was, but I thought I could go home in a few days. I called my mother to let her know I was okay.

Back at Dawn's house, the news was on: The fire updates were terrifying. I sat on the couch, watching in horror. I waited in silence until Jim came in. (He had both our bathrobes – thinking we would be home in a couple of days). He made to decision to go to Yreka where we could stay with his ex-wife and son for a few days. The reality of what I could have lost if my house was gone hit me as we went to Wal-Mart to get a few necessities. As we were purchasing toiletries, pajamas, underwear, hair brushes, etc. I wanted to scream. All I now owned was on my back and in 1 plastic bag.

We were in limbo for the next day and a half, not knowing the status of our home. Then we got the text that our house was gone.

THE ROAD TO RECOVERY AND BEYOND

"It isn't what happens to us that causes distress; it is how we react to what is happening to us."

I don't remember reacting to the news. I do remember buying a laptop and printer right way. I remember going to our Insurance Company and starting the paperwork for the claim. I remember trying to list every item that was in the house and figuring out the value of each one. The amount of paperwork was overwhelming. I also had to apply for a new passport, birth certificate, green card, and university transcripts. I still had no idea about the status of my car which I had left at the school parking lot.

Now that we knew we were homeless, it was "what next?" Where do we locate? We had no idea of where to live. We drove to different locations in Northern California such as Redding, but the houses were too expensive for us. Again, we were in limbo. We did not want to return to Southern California so that was not an option.

I finally found a mobile in Medford. It was in a nice park and it was perfect for us. Jim grudgingly agreed that we would purchase it and I signed the papers. I know Jim did not want to end up in another mobile home park; he wanted a place with a nice yard and a garage. I probably jumped the gun in insisting that we buy the place, but I kept thinking that we could pay cash for it and we would not have a heavy mortgage payment again, plus being heavily in debt. So, yes, I went against his wishes. I still feel guilty about his decision; however, it is so freeing not to be heavily in debt for the first time in my life. He decided to go back to Southern California to work for a month.. I spent the next 2 weeks buying furniture, household items, and food. In the meantime I had to have my toe operated on and wasn't able to walk for a couple of days.

I moved into the house on December 8. On December 10, I had to drive to Sacramento to get fingerprinted for my replacement green card. I spent the next couple of weeks shopping and reflecting on the move to Medford. I felt totally isolated. Our friends, Bonnie and Ken, had relocated nearby so that was a blessing. They had lost their home in Paradise also. But now I was faced with finding doctors, dentists, hairdresser, insurance. Also, I didn't know if I wanted to work again.

I was able to find a beautiful used antique desk and bookcase at an online garage sale. The husband delivered them to my house that same evening and even donated Christmas decorations to me. I found that many of the clerks in the stores were just as generous and kind. I got discounts on so many things. Instead of just accumulating belongs, I cherished the actions of those who help me find what I "needed".

I thought of the irony of my situation. I had been a totally organized person, always planning for the future. In Paradise, I had a year's supply of paper goods, non-perishable items, earthquake preparations, and first aid kits. I had mapped out our finances and budget. I was practicing the art of "letting go", realizing that I had many attachments to my wardrobe and belongings. Now, I could truly practice detachment – what is in my home are just furnishings; there is no emotional attachment to them. I was not consumed with buying jewelry and accessories. I did not have to cover every wall with pictures, to fill every space in the rooms. I was striving for simplicity. In fact, even now, our spare room is still empty. There is no furniture or pictures and I am okay with that. I do not know what I want to do with the room, and it is okay just to close the door to the room for the time being.

Monday, December 17: Bonnie and Ken drove me to Magalia to check on my car: It was still in the parking lot of the school, untouched by fire or smoke. I made the comment that I am truly rich: Jim and are back to being a two car family! Driving through Paradise was a painful experience: the entire town looked like a war zone. Hundreds of scorched cars scattered the landscapes. So many businesses and homes burnt to the ground. As I approached my cul-de sac, I burst into tears. There was not one house standing; there was nothing but ash on each lot. I leaned against my car, sobbing for a half an hour. I then drove by the shop where Jim was supposed to work. That, too was burnt to the ground. Jim's dreams for gainful employment had gone up in flames.

I thought about the emotional impact of the fire as I drove back to Medford. Jim never did recover completely from it. Paradise was his dream; working again was his therapy. He was angry and he sucked up all of the negative feelings. This was taking a toll on his body: his neck was so painful that he couldn't turn it and it affect his sleeping patterns. He was constantly in pain. We were both living in an area which was not our dream location and we still felt isolated as the only people we knew were our two friends from Paradise.

December 23: I picked Jim up at Sacramento and we went to his daughter's place in Folsom. I could believe the generosity of her family! She got me a beautiful photo blanket of Jim's family, many pairs of leggings and tops. We made it home for Christmas Eve – I had bought a tree and decorations Jim bought me a beautiful Buddha fountain for my office. Christmas was bittersweet as we weren't able to go home without passports or my green card.

The next few weeks were just a blur to me: Every day I would make phone calls to the insurance company, to the Passport Office, and other agencies. Still there was so much paperwork.

I decided that I need to work so I applied for a substitute teaching job. Again, more paperwork – all kinds of forms and I had to study for the Oregon Civil Rights Test! I had to make appointments to get my blood tested and get fingerprinted. I kept ignoring the pressure I was under until I finally collapsed. I fainted at a gas station on January 4. I fractured my arm and had deep abrasions.

On January 17, Jim left once again for Southern California. I spent the time, reading and meditating. I passed the Civil Rights Test and also the written Oregon Driving test!

On January 24, a hit an run driver crashed into our home and destroyed the skirting and some of the paneling. I was in the living room when it happened. It felt like a jolt from an earthquake. I filled out the incident report knowing that we would never be compensated for the damages. The next week I had both big toes operated on and was off my feet again.

I started teaching at the end of January! I kept busy over the next few weeks – the paperwork still building up. Jim retuned at the end of February. We settled into a comfortable routine: We would get up early in the morning and have coffee on the back deck. While I go ready for work, he would make my lunch, and then walk me to the car. He was (and still is) a Godsend. He does the grocery shopping and makes dinner (I never was a "Susie Homemaker" and he is a great cook!). I do the cleaning up and the laundry. I was kept busy during this time, with no time to reflect on anything. Had nightmares at night – flames coming at me, and I was beginning to have many mood swings. I kept up with my journal writing, but I was unable to meditate – my mind was so scattered. Felt out of sorts and it was hard to catch my breath.

April 1 – I went to Urgent Care: I had horrible chest pains and couldn't breathe. They put me in an ambulance and I was admitted to the hospital with double pneumonia. I couldn't believe the care I got in the hospital! The nurses were not only efficient, but caring. On April 13, I had a follow up visit with the doctor who was really concerned about me. He prescribed sleeping pills, anti-depressants and made an appointment with a psychologist.

RECOVERY AND TRANSFORMATION

So now the process of truly healing began. With the temporary help of the pills and the psychologist, I embraced my inner strength. I immersed myself into the readings of Deepak Chopra, the Dahli Lama, Bruce Lee, Miguel Ruiz, Wayne Dyer, Esther Hicks and Neville Goddard – to name a few. I took copious notes and practiced mindfulness and living in the now. Letting go has been truly freeing for me – not just of possessions, but of negative feelings and resentment. (The heart suffers the mind's distress – Deepak). The pleasure of getting things is so fleeting.

The road to my recovery has been a bumpy one. I had bouts of depression, harbored feelings of anger and resentment, and self-doubt. Yes, there were times when I just wanted to give up and times when I didn't think I could make it. But I would force myself to lean on my favorite authors, and glean some insights to keep going.

I found that all my authors had so much in common. The common ground was living in the now, appreciating our existence, being grateful for everything we have. Life isn't about possessions or appearances. It's about simplicity and only having what we need. It's about letting go.

I used read about letting go but now I was forced to let go. "Knowledge is useless until it gets activated" (Deepak Chopra") I was forced into a life of simplicity. I can witness what is going on around me from a detached position – I no longer have to try to control the details of my life. This frees me to be open- minded and not view life from a limited perspective. Bruce Lee uses the example of a cup -its usefulness is its emptiness. A closed (full) mind cannot take in any new information. An empty mind is essential to thriving.

I no longer have to identify myself by my titles (Professor/Counselor/ Teacher). I do not have to display my possessions. I am just "me" an evolving being embracing each day not knowing what tomorrow will bring. The Dahli Lama advises us that we need to hide our good qualities and achievements like a lamp inside a vessel. We are not to advertise them. This was difficult for me to do; now I realize the importance of being humble. This frees me up to truly listen to others, without judging or interjecting with what I am doing.

In June I turned 70 and was amazed at how good I felt emotionally and physically. I had recently joined the gym and made sure I worked out every day for at least an hour. I changed my eating habits to include as much fruit as possible, and to incorporate smoothies into my diet.

I have become a very frugal person. I pride myself at not doing any impulse shopping. I do not eat a t fast-food places, and I constantly put monies into the savings account. I am not concerned about my financial future; everything will take care of itself. I have everything I need so I do not need to accumulate "stuff" just because there is a huge sale going on! Before, I had to buy things because there was a sale and I would gloat about all the money I saved.

I am grateful to be healthy, to have a comfortable home, to be gainfully employed, to have a partner who is my rock and staunch supporter, and to have the support from dear friends and my mother.

The person before the fire was insecure, hiding behind possessions and titles. I am so blessed to have left that person in the ashes which allowed me to rise up from them.

Printed in the United States
By Bookmasters